The

FREEDOM
JOURNAL

Silencing the Critic to
Free Yourself for Possibility

DR. JACKIE ELDRIDGE

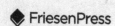 FriesenPress

One Printers Way,
Altona MB, R0G 0B0
Canada

www.friesenpress.com

ISBN
978-1-03-910898-1 (Hardcover)
978-1-03-910897-4 (Paperback)
978-1-03-910899-8 (eBook)

1. Self-Help, Journaling

Distributed to the trade by The Ingram Book Company

~DEDICATION~

This book is dedicated to all people who are seeking to understand themselves and others so they can contribute to making the world a kinder and more authentic place.

To Melanie Scott, you held my hand and my heart through the challenge that led to this book and championed this work every step of the way. You are awesome! Thank you!

To Sophia, Ranya, Allyson, Danika, Laurine, Judy , Denise, Beth and Matt, you gave me the gift of your time and your feedback was amazing. It really helped shape my thinking.

Thank you!

Fire Alarm

When you have pain in your life you automatically tense up.
You resist the pain or you fight it.
Unfortunately, that just makes the pain hang around.

Through experience you learn that the way out of pain
is not to resist it but to accept it.

One way you can begin to accept it is to see the pain
not as an attack on you or as a punishment of you,
but as a communication that tells you something is awry.

It is like a fire alarm that wakes you
before the fire engulfs you.
It is a messenger telling you to adjust something in your life
that is dysfunctional and out of balance.

~Paul Ferrini~

SHHHHH....

Most people do not like their thoughts and feelings to be criticized or worse, shut down. It often feels like we are being shooshed. Shooshing takes several forms: sometimes there is an actual finger to the lips "shhhh" aend other times there is a person "shooshing" you with their biting words of criticism. In both of these scenarios we feel exceedingly disrespected and demoralized.

We tell ourselves that the critic is simply rude and lacking empathy. We try not to take it personally and yet the feeling of being "shooshed" triggers our inner child and sends us reeling into self-doubt. We hear our inner saboteurs screaming, "You don't deserve to be heard" or "You are not worthy".

At other times, there is no other person involved. It is our own ravaging inner critic, the one with the death grip on our self-esteem. This all-too-familiar fault-finder is that inner voice who constantly seems to be stalking us from deep inside the darkness of our own minds.

This reflective journal is designed to help you turn the tables on these soul-sucking gremlins so that you regain your power, rise above your denigrators and find the true beauty of who you genuinely are. Through authentic reflection you are going to find your inner wisdom to re-write that old worthless script, transforming yourself into a strong and confident individual who will never again be "shooshed."

If you focus on the hurt, you will continue to suffer.
If you focus on the lesson, you will continue to grow.

~Buddha~

TABLE OF CONTENTS

ORIGINS OF THE
FREEDOM JOURNAL

I created *The Freedom Journal: Silencing the Critic to Free Yourself to Possibility* after I finally realized that I needed to speak up for myself and place limits on a long-term friendship that had been one of loose boundaries, censures, and advantage-taking.

In this relationship, I bent over backwards to please and accommodate; I was a life-long people-pleaser afraid of rocking the boat. I didn't want to make waves as I was terrified of losing this person in my life and so I just sat back and listened whenever I was criticized. I would smile and nod my head but inside my guts churned and my throat constricted as I sat in silence not able to give voice to what I was truly thinking and feeling.

Then one day, I knew I had reached my limit. My critic crossed a line that shattered my core values and fragmented my belief about who I knew myself to be. I could no longer listen to this incessant disapproving voice nor any other for that matter. I had plenty of my own internal voices threatening my self-perception. I certainly didn't need someone else to get in on that losing game.

Through reflection and personal examination, I began to notice something shifting deep inside and I knew I was ready to stand up for myself! I realized it was time to let people know it was not acceptable to pass judgement and I would no longer sit back and just take it as though the arrows flung my way never pierced my heart.

I was ready and prepared.... or so I thought. Sadly, all of my preparation did not serve me in this particular circumstance. Instead, when I spoke up my critic came at me with the vengeance of a painfully scorned lover, pulling out the cruelty of a person solely intent on revenge. Instead of continuing to stand my ground and using my voice, I immediately dissolved into a murky puddle of self-doubt as I did a deep dive into a sink hole of low self-esteem and feelings of unworthiness.

I stayed in this dark place for several weeks until I finally saw a glimmer of light and hope with the help of a true and knowledgeable friend. With this new-found illumination, I examined that fateful exchange from every possible angle and I could not find one reason why any criticism of me was warranted. I was simply creating a boundary that should have been done many years before. I was worn out with analysis and I had grown weary of being disparaged. I knew that this empty place of despair was not serving me and so I began to write.

I journaled my thoughts and feelings and then I voraciously wrote out the criticisms so that I could be crystal clear what they actually were; empty words spoken by someone who is deeply wounded and grasping for someone else to harm in order to raise themself up.

It is not easy for us to get to a place where we can see the other person's intent or needs but it is critical to find our own inner strength and wisdom. We all have it; we just need to find the signposts to begin the journey towards reclamation of our true selves.

The Freedom Journal is meant to provide you with a tool that will shine light on the harmful messages we hear from others or that we tell ourselves. Once they are illuminated, we can understand that these messages are highly destructive and they rob us of the ability to see the radiance that shines our way to new opportunity. When our light is blurred or extinguished, we feel trapped. Sometimes this feeling is temporary and yet it can also be all-consuming and long-lasting.

The Freedom Journal is only one tool. You must be mindful of whether this tool is enough to move you forward or whether you might need additional help in the form of a coach or therapist. Many people have difficulty asking for help because their inner critic is telling them they are weak or unworthy but it is actually a sign of strength since you have a solid understanding of what is needed to move forward. If you need additional tools never be afraid to ask for them!

While the relationship I spoke about did not survive, I am confident that I overcame the demons that had long-held me prisoner. I learned a great deal about myself through this process and I was able to move on with a clear sense about creating boundaries and respecting myself. I was also able to reach a place of forgiveness which deepened my sense of freedom.

THE MODUS OPERANDI
OF THE CRITIC

*The more we refuse to buy into our inner
critics - and our external ones too - the easier
it will get to have confidence in our choices,
and to feel comfortable with who we are.*

~Arianna Huffington~

We all experience both inner and outer critics. It is a consequence of living in a world filled with differing experiences, perspectives and beliefs. Social media has only served to exacerbate the problem in so many ways. In fact, put downs are rampant in our society and have become the norm. Many think they are desensitized but the truth is they are not. The words still cut to the core and can send us reeling. Our inner critic is often quick to judge by telling us we are stupid, ugly, fat, unworthy, undeserving, not qualified, mean...the list goes on and on and on!

This inner critic can be relentless and if we are not careful, it can prevent us from living our lives to the fullest. It can block us from moving forward, keeping us stuck in the belief that we are never good enough. This soul detractor often starts the all-too-familiar diatribe first thing in the morning as soon as we look in the mirror. If our inner critic has a stronghold on us then we automatically start our day being sabotaged by this disapproving voice. We don't stand a chance against this opponent and so we begin the day, sometimes unconsciously uncovering evidence that the critic may actually be right.

As if the inner critic is not painful enough, we also experience outer critics, people who cannot resist putting us down, attempting to keep us in our place. This outer critic often lacks self-esteem and feels they must put us down in order to build themselves up. Others have an overdeveloped sense of self, feeling compelled to share their wisdom because, of course, they know best.

Regardless of the modus operandi of the outer critic they often hold power over us because their words are hurtful and frequently trigger our inner child and our inner critic and all of the feelings of shame, unworthiness, anger and fear that reside deep within us.

People who constantly criticize often feel threatened by us or they view themselves in competition with us. They are trying to intimidate us by making themselves feel more dominant. While this critic may be vicious in their attack, they, themselves, are often experiencing deep and unresolved feelings of fear, hurt, rejection and unworthiness.

However, not every outer critic demonstrates this malicious kind of criticism. Instead, they may actually believe they are being helpful by giving us feedback in order to help us improve. In this case, we must allow ourselves to look beneath the surface of the criticism and deep into the spirit of the critic in order to uncover their intent all the while establishing healthy boundaries for ourselves.

As we begin this journey towards silencing our critics, it is important to reflect on our mindset so we can open ourselves up to possibility. Many of our beliefs stem from being locked into fixed vs. growth mindsets. When our beliefs about ourselves are fixed, the critic has a definite edge. If our mindset is fixed, we may be unconsciously attracting criticism because we do not believe we are worthy or we can't do certain things. But we are and we can! It's all about perspective! We will succeed when we open our minds.

As you are going through this process and reflecting on your experiences, be very vigilant about your mindset. Catch yourself when you see that you are working from a fixed mindset. Learning to change is about growing. Giving yourself affirmations and showing gratitude will also help change your mindset, helping you to see the positive instead of always dwelling in the negative. The following chart will help you understand this concept.

Fixed Mindset

- I can't do this
- I give up
- This is too hard for me
- I keep making mistakes
- I am not worthy
- I am so stupid
- No one cares about me

Growth Mindset

- I am going to keep trying
- I will try a different strategy
- It may take more time to learn
- I will learn from my mistakes
- Everyone is worthy of love and respect
- I have succeeded this far and I keep learning
- I am a good person and there are people who care. I will accept that

As all of us are only too aware, the loud and frantic voices of the outer world easily drown out the small, still loving voice within.
~Marianne Williamson~

WHY SHOULD I WORK TO SILENCE THE CRITIC?

Don't get attached to any words.
They are only stepping stones.

~Eckhart Tolle~

Emotional Intelligence (EQ) is thought to be the highest indicator of success and so, it is important for us to understand what nurtures our EQ and also what we are doing to break it down. When we have a high degree of emotional intelligence, we are able to face our critics because we are self-aware and able to distinguish between the truth about ourselves and the destructive messages of our real or perceived demons. But the critic is unconcerned with our emotional intelligence since they do not possess a high degree of their own. In actual fact, they have very little self-awareness because they do not care about (or fail to see) the negative impact their words and actions have on others. Instead, they believe they have every right to criticize and demean. When people crumble because of their words they view it as a win for them. They imagine they have full power.

When we, ourselves, are not self-aware or able to express our thoughts and feelings, we are at risk of being emotionally destroyed by the critic. If we are in a weakened state, we are vulnerable. It is during these times that we believe the nasty faultfinder; doubting ourselves and getting stuck in a quagmire of low self-esteem. Becoming attached to this uncertainty can lead to a great deal of emotional pain and even depression.

As we have already established, we all have critics, both inner and outer. We also float in and out of listening to the critic. A high degree of emotional intelligence will protect us to a degree but we are human and we sometimes let our guard down allowing the critic to get inside our heads.

"Shooshing" our critics is one way of nurturing our emotional intelligence enabling us to grow and move forward in fulfilling our life's desire and purpose. When the saboteurs have been put to rest, we can see ourselves clearly, embracing our strengths and truly understanding who we are and where we are going.

"Shooshing" also gives us permission to set boundaries between us and others. People do not have the right to criticize us and yet we do not always shut down the comments. Learning to "shhhh" is crucial and yet we must learn to quiet the critic mindfully. We cannot meet our critics with anger even when they come at us from this position. Doing so will only provoke the critic as happened with me. When we "shhhh" skillfully it sends the message to our critics that we are no longer going to accept their disrespect. It also sends the message that we value ourselves and that we command respect.

Setting boundaries with our outer critics is not an easy task and yet it is manageable through our words and actions. We can speak the words that hold our critics at bay but the same cannot be said for our inner critic.

With our own personal demons, there is no physical presence with whom we are conversing. The voices are in our heads. By virtue of this fact alone we can be more challenged by our inner critic. If we do not clear our minds of these voices, they will find a way to continue to torture us in their attempts to get us to believe their unfounded and soul-destroying messages. When the critic is allowed to take up residence in our minds, we feed it and that power will limit us by keeping us the prisoner of our thoughts. We must find a way to eliminate the critic's voice.

Being free of the critic opens doors to possibility as we begin to see clearly that we are not the words we, or others, are telling us. It is our perception and not our reality.

Of course, there is always the danger that we will alienate our outer critic and they may choose to walk away. It happens, and then we must ask ourselves if that is such a bad thing. Our self-protection is crucial for self-growth and saying good-bye to a critic may be the answer to finding the freedom we seek.

I dwell in possibility.
~Emily Dickinson~

MINDFULNESS

Mindfulness helps us freeze the frame so that we can become aware of our sensations and experiences as they are, without the distorting coloration of socially conditioned responses or habitual reactions.

~Henepola Gunaratana~

Mindfulness practice is important in all aspects of our lives. It helps us to see the world more clearly and enables us to remain calm in the face of challenges. Mindfulness moves us from the sympathetic nervous system (SNS – the centre for fight, flight or freeze) to our parasympathetic nervous system (PNS) which promotes healing, regeneration, nourishment of the body and regulation of the immune system. The PNS is aroused by feelings of calm, love, peacefulness, contentment, satisfaction and appreciation.

It will be very helpful to spend a few mindful moments before starting your journal so that you are open to possibility. Doing so will reduce the emotional high-jacking that you may be experience as you continually listen to the critic.

Starting a daily practice can be one of the hardest parts of your mindfulness journey. We are creatures of habit and sometimes staying the course with our old ways can be a comfortable place even though we know things have to change for us.

A new beginning is often riddled with excuses as to why we can't start or why we must abandon our attempts at continuing a course of action that we ultimately know will be good for us. Here is a place where your inner critic is going to actively try to prevent you from embracing mindfulness by claiming "You will never be able to do this, you have monkey mind", "You are stupid if you think this will work".

While you may have some evidence to support these claims if you have tried mindfulness and not met with success, there is a myriad of evidence to prove that you can and will succeed if you set your intention. Be gentle with yourself here. Take baby steps.

I have sometimes lost my practice during high periods of stress and yet I always know it is there. When I get back to mindfulness, I will be able to move forward by working with what is in the present moment. I do not beat myself up for being human. I simply begin again.

Mindfulness is about love and loving life.
When you cultivate this love, it gives you
clarity and compassion for life, and your
actions happen in accordance with that.

~Jon Kabat-Zinn~

TOOLS TO "SILENCE"
THE CRITIC?

There are no secrets to success. It is the result of
preparation, hard work, and learning from failure.

~Colin Powell~

Reflection is the first step in silencing the critic. Using this journal is a step-by-step process that provides insight into the messages we are hearing from our critics through a visual record of the actual or imaginary conversations in which we are engaged. It then guides us through the process of rewriting the script and helps us to acknowledge the impact we want to have in the world once we are free. The process is liberating and unclutters our minds so that we can see possibility.

As you work through the journal you will begin to see patterns. Pay attention to them! You will recognize the same voice popping up in a variety of situations. You will also begin to feel less attached to the critic and more confident in your abilities to quiet that disrespectful voice.

You will likely take note of the criticism either in the moment or after you have had time to reflect on the conversation you had. Until we become more adept at catching them, critical comments can sneak past us until later when we have time to think it all through. Be mindful and listen attentively. For example:

Critic's Comment

- You are insensitive
- You are stupid

Whenever we experience a dissonant thought such as condemnation, we also feel that concept in our bodies. Being aware of our body's reaction is extremely helpful to us as there is a lot of important information contained in this mind/body connection. First of all, our body is sending us a signal that we need to pay attention to something. It is also warning us that this experience is stressful and, if left unacknowledged, it will remain in our body with the potential of causing us ill-health. The body is creating a space for new learning and is sending you a powerful message that must not be ignored. Where does criticism reside in your body? For example:

Body Connection

- Chest pain
- Throat constriction

While our critic has used words or phrases against us, there is often a hidden missive that we interpret. The content may be fact or fiction. It is most often the latter. This message can destroy us if it is left unchecked. It serves to reinforce our already faulty belief system and can cause us to sink deeper and deeper into low self-esteem. At its worst, it can propel us into depression as our thoughts become darker and darker and the hole where we find ourselves becomes deeper. We must ask ourselves what it is that we heard? For example:

Perceived Message

- I am a bad person
- I am not worthy

You will begin to understand that there is often little evidence to support your critic's accusations. Your critic has planted an insidious seed that is designed to throw you off balance. It is only through your honest reflection that you can refuse to let it tip you over.

However, you might begin to see that there may be a tiny bit of evidence to back up their claim. It might be something that you did that one time during an emotional high-jacking. When this realization occurs, it is because there can, sometimes, be grains of truth in what is being said. Realizing this fact can be an extremely hard pill to swallow and can further high-jack us if we are not fully awake. Recovering from this commandeering can be challenging. However, it is important to understand that this realization is simply a setback. Instead of wallowing in self-pity, we can choose to learn from this grain of truth as we rewrite the script so that our impact in the world is even greater. For example:

Evidence For

- I have occasionally made an insensitive comment when I felt stressed
- I did not know the answer

When we look at the evidence for or against, we must look deeper to find out what message we need to hear in order to reach our full potential. When we look for and find the meaning in our new-found knowledge we can more easily let go of the hurt. We begin to see more clearly and we understand that our critic is ill-informed. They do not really know who we are beyond their perception. Our new learning is motivational and it gives us courage. We begin to understand there is another script that we can follow as we "shhhh" our critics.

Look deep and find the evidence that demonstrates you are not the person you are being told you are. The proof is there, unearth it and make sure you let it sink in deeply. It is far more accurate than your saboteur is leading you to believe. For example:

Evidence Against

- People often tell me I am very sensitive to others
- I am regularly praised for my informed contributions and knowledge

In every experience, there will always be learning, no matter how challenging the event. Pay close attention. Is your critic telling you that you "always" do something or you "never" do? These words are emotionally charged and designed to incite you. You "should" or "shouldn't" fall under the same category. They imply obligation and you are not obligated to behave in the ways your nemesis desires. Instead, learn for yourself because you are learning to be the best person you can be. It is not about pleasing them.

New Learning

- Sometimes people project their own insecurities on others
- I have been successful in my learning

Rewriting the script that the critic uses against us and examining our impact in the world are equally important steps. They make it crystal clear that we are not the person we are being told we are. We are much greater than that and we are destined to do amazing things.

Re-writing the Script

- I show my sensitivity by deeply listening to my friends when they need me
- I love to learn new things and I will continue to self-actualize

A further step beyond rewriting the script is understanding the impact that you want to have in the world. If we remain solely focused on ourselves, our learning stays somewhat superficial. When we step outside of ourselves and look at our potential influence, it deepens our resolve and empowers us to move forward. We become invested in our self-actualization. We all want to make a difference and so we must gain the wisdom and confidence to do so. Spend some time exploring what you want to contribute and then take the steps necessary to do so. Developing our social-responsibility is a sign post of emotional intelligence.

Impact I Want to Have in the World Today

- I want to show and model empathy for others to make the world a better place
- I want to model life-long learning

Reflection and clarity are crucial and the next step is equally, if not more important. This additional phase moves us forward to even greater heights and sets us up for more fulfillment as we journey through our lives. After exploring our critic's message, the learning we now have and rewriting our scripts, we also need to express gratitude. While expressing gratitude to someone who has put us down may seem counter-intuitive, it is actually liberating because they have taught us some important lessons.

You can't let criticism stop you
from learning new things.
~Joe Buck~

GRATITUDE

Gratitude is the healthiest of all human emotions. The more you express gratitude for what you have, the more likely you will have even more to express gratitude for.

~Zig Ziglar~

There is a great deal of attention being paid to gratitude these days. The cultivation of daily gratitude increases our emotional intelligence, happiness and well-being. When we express and deeply feel gratitude, we are actually embracing life and hope. We are moving outside of ourselves into the relationships we have with others. Gratitude fosters optimism, joy and a sense of self-control. It also moves us into the parasympathetic nervous system where we are less likely to feel stress.

When we are able to silence our critics, expressing gratitude deepens the experience. Reflection on the learning we gain from our experience with our critic and feeling gratitude for this new-found knowledge propels us to clear "self" and "other" awareness. We no longer see ourselves as being separate; instead we are able to see how we are all connected. We are more able to move away from the self-centred mindset where we potentially see people as "other," to a healthier mindset that we are part of a collective whole. Consequently, we are able to set healthy boundaries with our inner and outer critics.

Daily Gratitude

- I am thankful for my family and friends
- I have gratitude for the abundance of knowledge I gained

Gratitude makes sense of our past, brings peace for today, and creates a vision for tomorrow.

~Melodie Beattie~

DAILY AFFIRMATIONS

By affirming your own gifts and accomplishments,
you build your confidence and increase
your ability to build a brighter future.
~Debbie Ford~

Our first step has been to uncover the critic, exposing them for who they really are. Following this exposure, we examine the learning so we can rewrite the script, understanding how we can make a greater impact in the world. Our next step is to express gratitude so that we create space to open our hearts. We are opening to others and, by extension, to ourselves.

These actions are valuable and necessary if we have any hope of silencing our critics. Each and every time we hear the critic, we can reflect using the journal, enabling us to see our thoughts and realize that we are not them.

There, is however, one additional step that will further integrate our learning so that we are better equipped to take on this task. Daily affirmations solidify our knowledge and they keep us in a place of self-knowing. When spoken or read daily, we immerse ourselves in the new thoughts and they become a part of us. Our thoughts contribute to our forward action and they help us to believe we can and will succeed.

In my experience, having affirmations on my computer or above my desk work for a while. But soon they simply become wallpaper and I stop seeing them. However, when I write them out each day, I am actively engaged in my learning and they stick with me a lot longer.

Daily Affirmation

- I am a sensitive and caring person who will make a difference in the world
- I am intelligent

It's the repetition of affirmations that leads to belief. And once that belief becomes a deep conviction, things begin to happen.

~Muhammad Ali~

FORGIVENESS

Keep in mind that forgiving is not for others. It is for you. Forgiving is not forgetting. It is remembering without anger. It frees up your power, heals your body, mind and spirit. Forgiveness opens up a pathway to a new place of peace where you can persist despite what has happened to you.

~Les Brown~

I frequently hear people say, "I just can't forgive. They caused me too much pain". This belief is common and yet it will only serve to keep us stuck in the challenging emotions that are associated with the act requiring clemency. However, there is tremendous value in finding your way through the darkness to the light of forgiveness.

You do not actually have to see the person face-to-face to forgive. You may have decided the person will no longer be part of your life. That is fine. This compassion can simply be a still place in your heart.

While forgiving others is often challenging, self-forgiveness can seem almost out-of-reach for many of us. However, we must strive for this goal as it leads us towards self-love and compassion. It is the very thing that will help us get in touch with our inner child who is oftentimes wounded and now reacting negatively to the voices of our inner and outer critics.

It is helpful to sit in Loving Kindness meditation to reach a place of forgiveness because it opens your heart to yourself and others.

Loving Kindness (Metta) is an ancient Buddhist meditation leading to the development of unconditional loving-kindness and friendliness. "Metta" is something you feel in your heart, a positive emotional state towards others as well as ourselves. As a result of practising Metta, we become more empathetic, considerate, kind, forgiving, and in general, more loving, friendly people.

Metta practice helps us:

- Develop our emotional intelligence.
- Develop resilience.
- Bring harmony into our lives and in our relationships.
- Rid ourselves of internal and external conflicts.
- Overcome lacerating guilt.
- Be open to loving acceptance of ourselves and others.
- Deepen our connections with all beings.
- Cope with stresses that are present in the world, especially as we are often inundated with traumatic news events that we are powerless to change.
- Move towards forgiveness.

To Practise:

- Bring your awareness to your heart centre by noticing the beating of your heart and realizing the life-giving force that it provides.

- Bring someone or something (a pet) who has given you unconditional love into your awareness – notice all feelings associated with that unconditional love. Here is a good time to make the mind-body-spirit connection.

- Now take those feelings and bring them to each of the following one at a time: family and friends; co-workers; people in your neighbourhood; people in your city, in your province/state, in your country, in the world. Each time you move to a different person or group of people you will take the time to really feel that loving kindness throughout every aspect of your being. It is important to really feel it.

- Now bring your loving kindness awareness back to yourself – feeling the love you have shared and surrounding yourself in that love. Breathe it in, feel it in your mind-body-spirit.

- Take the time to soak in that loving kindness towards yourself and know that you are worthy of being loved.

- Practise daily loving kindness, especially towards yourself. You might find it helpful to remember the "oxygen mask" metaphor. You must put your mask on first in order to be able to look after others.

When others have hurt you, you have a choice. You can carry that hurt/anger with you, letting it eat away at you or you can send loving kindness to that person and work towards forgiveness. Forgiveness is generally not about the person you are forgiving; it is about freedom for yourself.

To forgive is to set a prisoner free and
discover that the prisoner was you.
~Lewis B. Smedes~

SETTING MY INTENTION

*Like real seeds, intentions can't grow if you
hold on to them. Only when you release your
intentions into the fertile depths of your
consciousness can they grow and flourish.*

~Deepak Chopra~

The act of setting intentions is the way we get things done.
When we need to buy groceries, we make a list, thereby setting
the intention to pick up the food we require. When we decide
that we want a healthier lifestyle, we set our intention to: join
a gym, hire a trainer, go on a diet. Setting the intention is easy.
Sticking to it is the challenge. The Upanishads teach us:

> You are what your deepest desire is. As your
> desire is, so is your intention. As your inten-
> tion is, so is your will. As your will is, so is your
> deed. As your deed is, so is your destiny.

Before beginning *The Freedom Journal*, firmly set your intention for quieting your critics and healing the scars that have

been left by them. You are also setting the intention to change your story so that you will be stronger in facing the critics as you move through the landscape of your life. You may have other intentions for taking this journey. This expedition is a personal one and you must consider your individual intentions.

There is, however, a caution with setting intentions. What happens if we waiver? What happens if we don't follow through? Well, your inner critic is going to embrace the opportunity to jump in and start sabotaging you for not moving forward. They are lying in wait for you to fail.

The fact is, we all have setbacks and they happen for various reasons. If you experience an obstacle don't resist it, savor it. Use it as an opening to understand your critic. Make use of the journal to help you to understand why you wandered away from the intention. Examine your intention and then set it again!

The most important aspect of setting the intention is providing the space for the intention to sink deep into our being. We want to integrate the intention to our conscious awareness so that we become committed to the possibilities in front of us.

One way of allowing them to become fully integrated is to review your plans at night before you drop off to sleep. Perhaps, you read them over or put them on a vision board that you see before closing your eyes. This simple action will begin to implant the ideas in your unconscious mind and help you to act more fervently.

*It's amazing how much you can learn if
your intentions are truly earnest.*

~Chuck Berry~

ACCOUNTABILITY

*You are responsible for your life. If you're sitting
around waiting on somebody to save you, to fix you,
to even help you, you are wasting your time. Only
you have the power to move your life forward.*

~Oprah Winfrey~

Oprah's quote is crucial for us to understand. We are all indi-
vidually responsible for ourselves. There are many times when
we prefer to work through our personal challenges alone, free
of the possibility of criticism of those who may/may not be
judging us. This preference may also be the voice of our inner
critic: fear of what people think, shame, guilt and on and on.
However, we also know that keeping our negative messages
and thoughts to ourselves is a recipe for disaster because these
demons like to stay safely tucked away in our imaginations and
in our bodies.

Designing an alliance of accountability with a trusted friend,
coach or therapist allows us to openly express our thoughts
and emotions thereby releasing them from our minds. When

we liberate ourselves in this way, there is a power shift. The thoughts and emotions are no longer governing us. Instead, we are controlling our reactions to them and we are, indeed, changing the story and dwelling in possibility.

Enlisting an accountability buddy, while working through *The Freedom Journal*, keeps us on track. We might check in with our accountability buddy from time-to-time just to let them know we are actually filling in the journal and examining our thoughts and emotions. Or, we may check in with them sharing our actual reflections thereby deepening the learning. The way you enroll an accountability buddy is your choice. There is no right or wrong way. It has to work for you in order for you to stay the course.

It is, however, important to know that the right person will hold space for you to grow. You will want to set a boundary by letting them know you need a safe and nurturing friend who is there to support you and **not criticize** you. Creating this collaborative space is actually an assertive act as you are learning these new skills. This step is an important one because you already know that you need to set boundaries with your critics.

Find the right person you can trust!

Maybe you're not perfect, but you're willing to actually look at yourself and take some kind of accountability. That's a change. It might not mean that you can turn everything around, but I think there's something incredibly hopeful about that.

~Brie Larson~

GETTING STARTED

The secret of getting ahead is getting started.

~Mark Twain~

Staying stuck in old habits can, sometimes, feel safe even when we feel deeply disturbed by the experiences. It may seem strange that staying with the pain of criticism can somehow seem preferential over creating boundaries. The truth is the fear of change and standing up for oneself can be greater than just accepting our critics.

However, there is hope and possibility for taking charge and creating a new version of you; one who is strong, confident and ready to embrace life without critics sabotaging you at every turn.

The time is now...

*Realize deeply that the present moment
is all you ever have. Make the Now
the primary focus to your life.*

~Eckhart Tolle~

Most humans are never fully present
in the now, because unconsciously they
believe that the next moment must be more
important than this one. But then you miss
your whole life, which is never not now.

~Eckhart Tolle~

First, set your intention. What is it that you want to accomplish in your journal entries?

Setting an Intention

- I intend to look deeply and honestly into the perceived message(s) in order to understand the truth about myself.

- I intend to move forward in my life by freeing myself from criticism.

The next step is to claim an affirmation. The more you affirm yourself, the more esteem you will build. When you start *The Freedom Journal* with an affirmation, you are building a muscle that will help you hush your critic with confidence. You are also adding to the evidence that you are a good person who is creative, resourceful and whole. Note: the journal does not differentiate between inner and outer critics. As mentioned, it does not matter if they are real or imagined, their messages are ultimately harmful and damaging and they need to be stopped.

The journal has several sections that you will work through whenever you hear the voice(s) of your inner or outer critic(s). It is important to fill in each one and work through each concept to the end as you will begin to see patterns forming and you will experience the growth associated with this awareness.

If you are like many others who have inner critics, the voices happen every day, sometimes several times throughout this time frame. The more times you catch the critic the deeper your learning will be.

The time of day when you fill in the journal depends on when the critic's voice is the loudest. If looking in the mirror first thing in the morning triggers phrases like, "You are so stupid," "You are ugly," then take a few moments to go through the process as soon as possible.

If the critic is external, you will take the time to reflect right away, as soon as you hear a critical comment. You will want to remember the details as clearly as possible. There is a lot of merit in realizing the body connection. Remember, your body is also sending you a strong message.

Perhaps the most important piece of this reflection is honesty. You want to be factual. It is not about making yourself right and the critic wrong. It is about learning. It is about examining the evidence, re-writing the script and then realizing the impact you want to have in the world.

As you travel this path, you are going to find that you will begin to catch the critic sooner. Upon completion of your reflection, you will write one or more statements of gratitude. This step may be related to your reflection or it may be something else that you have gratitude for that is unrelated. Feeling gratitude after your reflection leaves you in a positive space instead of staying with any challenging emotions that may have arisen during your reflection. Staying in that negative space will cloud your growth, disempowering you to move ahead.

Martin Seligman, the father of Positive Psychology, encourages us to look for hope and gratitude when we find ourselves stuck. He reminds us that a positive attitude gives us strength and courage leading to lasting fulfillment, meaning and purpose.

This journal provides you with several opportunities for reflection to truly deepen your experience. You may notice that you conquer your critics sooner than that. You may find that quieting your inner critic is far simpler than silencing your outer critic. We are all individual in our needs and our abilities to grow. The bottom line is you need to be compassionate with yourself and give yourself whatever time you need. Affirm and believe in yourself. The following are two examples to get you started so you can fly!

> *Your Critics are waiting for you. Have*
> *courage... You got this!*
>
> *~Jackie Eldridge~*

*When you start to develop your powers of empathy
and imagination, the whole world opens up to you.*

~Susan Sarandon~

My Intention:

I intend to examine the times I express empathy.

Affirmation(s):

I am a kind and loving person who cares deeply for myself
and others.

Critic's Voice:

You lack empathy (Outer Critic)

Body Connection:

Chest pain, throat closing, stomach pain.

Perceived Message(s):

You are a bad person, you are cruel, people do not like you,
people will not want to be with you, you should not tell people
how their actions affect you

Possible Evidence For:

I stated my feelings at an inopportune time.

Evidence Against:

Many people comment on my empathy, I have asked for feedback from several people and received evidence to contradict the assumption that I am not empathetic, it is my highest score on my emotional intelligence assessment, it is part of my personality type.

New Learning:

I can ask for feedback to re-affirm my inner wisdom; people will be honest, keep reminding yourself about your strengths.

Rewriting the Script:

Empathy is a core value of mine and I will show empathy to the family and friends who will let me in, I will set healthy boundaries.

Impact I Want to have in the World Today:

Continue to be empathetic but with boundaries so that people don't take advantage.

Gratitude:

I have gratitude for my self-awareness and ability to seek answers.

You are responsible for what you believe, even
if you choose to believe what others tell you.

~Paul Ferrini~

My Intention:

Today I intend to listen to the lesson from my inner critic.

Affirmation(s):

I am a strong and intelligent woman.

Critic's Voice:

You are stupid (Inner Critic).

Body Connection:

Shoulder tension, tightness in chest.

Perceived Message:

You are not capable because you are stupid. You are not worthy.

Possible Evidence For:

My father repeatedly told me I was stupid when I was a child.

Evidence Against:

I have a doctoral degree, I teach at a university, people have told me they think I am smart.

New Learning:

Stay with the evidence against as it tells the real story.

Rewriting the Script:

I will continue to use my intelligence to move forward. I will continue to repeat my daily affirmations.

Impact I Want to have in the World Today:

I want to use my intelligence and passion to create materials that will help others who experience these critics.

Gratitude:

I have gratitude for the educational opportunities I have had.

*Creating time to reflect on your life could be
the key to reaching your greatest potential.*

~Amy Morin~

Now it's your turn to reflect, set intentions and give yourself the affirmations you deserve. It is also time to express your gratitude for all of the amazing things that have been part of your life.

This journal provides you with several opportunities for reflection to truly deepen your experience. Taking time is critical to really let the changes you are attempting to make sink in and become integrated into your new way of thinking and behaving.

You have likely had years of listening to the voice of that critic, and it will not be unlearned in a few short days. Be gentle with yourself, acknowledge your value and take the time that is needed.

You are worth it!

If we lose love and self-respect for each other, this is how we finally die.

~Maya Angelou~

My Intention:

_____

_____

_____

Affirmation(s):

_____

_____

_____

Critic's Voice:

_____

_____

_____

Body Connection:

_____

_____

_____

Perceived Message:

_____

_____

_____

Possible Evidence For:

_____

_____

_____

Evidence Against:

_____

_____

_____

New Learning:

_____

_____

_____

Rewriting the Script:

_____

_____

_____

Impact I Want to Have in the World Today:

_____

_____

_____

Gratitude:

_____

_____

_____

We're taught to be ashamed of confusion, anger, fear and sadness, and to me they're of equal value to happiness, excitement and inspiration.

~Alanis Morissette~

My Intention:

_____

_____

_____

Affirmation(s):

_____

_____

_____

Critic's Voice:

_____

_____

_____

Body Connection:

_____

_____

_____

Perceived Message:

_____

_____

_____

Possible Evidence For:

_____

_____

_____

Evidence Against:

_____

_____

_____

New Learning:

_____

_____

_____

Rewriting the Script:

_____

_____

_____

Impact I Want to Have in the World Today:

_____

_____

_____

Gratitude:

_____

_____

_____

Criticism may not be agreeable, but it is necessary. It fulfils the same function as pain in the human body. It calls attention to an unhealthy state of things.

~Winston Churchill~

My Intention:

_____

_____

_____

Affirmation(s):

_____

_____

_____

Critic's Voice:

_____

_____

_____

Body Connection:

_____

_____

_____

Perceived Message:

_____

_____

_____

Possible Evidence For:

_____

_____

_____

Evidence Against:

_____

_____

_____

New Learning:

_____

_____

_____

Rewriting the Script:

_____

_____

_____

Impact I Want to Have in the World Today:

_____

_____

_____

Gratitude:

_____

_____

_____

Between stimulus and response there is a space.
In that space is our power to choose our response.
In our response lies our growth and our freedom.

~Viktor E. Frankl~

My Intention:

_____

_____

_____

Affirmation(s):

_____

_____

_____

Critic's Voice:

_____

_____

_____

Body Connection:

_____

_____

_____

Perceived Message:

_____

_____

_____

Possible Evidence For:

_____

_____

_____

Evidence Against:

_____

_____

_____

New Learning:

_____

_____

_____

Rewriting the Script:

_____

_____

_____

Impact I Want to Have in the World Today:

_____

_____

_____

Gratitude:

_____

_____

_____

*Hard times arouse an instinctive
desire for authenticity.*

~ Coco Chanel ~

My Intention:

_____

_____

_____

Affirmation(s):

_____

_____

_____

Critic's Voice:

_____

_____

_____

Body Connection:

_____

_____

_____

Perceived Message:

_____

_____

_____

Possible Evidence For:

_____

_____

_____

Evidence Against:

_____

_____

_____

New Learning:

_____

_____

_____

Rewriting the Script:

_____

_____

_____

Impact I Want to Have in the World Today:

_____

_____

_____

Gratitude:

_____

_____

_____

Self-love is the source of all our other loves.

~Pierre Corneille~

My Intention:

_____

_____

_____

Affirmation(s):

_____

_____

_____

Critic's Voice:

_____

_____

_____

Body Connection:

_____

_____

_____

Perceived Message:

_____

_____

_____

Possible Evidence For:

_____

_____

_____

Evidence Against:

_____

_____

_____

New Learning:

_____

_____

_____

Rewriting the Script:

_____

_____

_____

Impact I Want to Have in the World Today:

_____

_____

_____

Gratitude:

_____

_____

_____

*Nurturing our capacity to be mindful and present is
the first step to understanding and disempowering
the identity and power of the inner critic.*

~Christina Feldman~

My Intention:

_____

_____

_____

Affirmation(s):

_____

_____

_____

Critic's Voice:

_____

_____

_____

Body Connection:

_____

_____

_____

Perceived Message:

_____

_____

_____

Possible Evidence For:

_____

_____

_____

Evidence Against:

_____

_____

_____

New Learning:

_____

_____

_____

Rewriting the Script:

_____

_____

_____

Impact I Want to Have in the World Today:

_____

_____

_____

Gratitude:

_____

_____

_____

Every lesson that comes into your life asks you
to open your heart and mind in a new way.

~Paul Ferrini~

My Intention:

_____

_____

_____

Affirmation(s):

_____

_____

_____

Critic's Voice:

_____

_____

_____

Body Connection:

_____

_____

_____

Perceived Message:

_____

_____

_____

Possible Evidence For:

_____

_____

_____

Evidence Against:

_____

_____

_____

New Learning:

_____

_____

_____

Rewriting the Script:

_____

_____

_____

Impact I Want to Have in the World Today:

_____

_____

_____

Gratitude:

_____

_____

_____

Believe you can and you're halfway there.

~Theodore Roosevelt~

My Intention:

_____

_____

_____

Affirmation(s):

_____

_____

_____

Critic's Voice:

_____

_____

_____

Body Connection:

_____

_____

_____

Perceived Message:

_____

_____

_____

Possible Evidence For:

_____

_____

_____

Evidence Against:

_____

_____

_____

New Learning:

_____

_____

_____

Rewriting the Script:

_____

_____

_____

Impact I Want to Have in the World Today:

_____

_____

_____

Gratitude:

_____

_____

_____

Whether you know it or not,
the only person you can attack is yourself.
You may believe that you are attacking someone else,
but that's just an illusion.

~Paul Ferrini~

My Intention:

_____

_____

_____

Affirmation(s):

_____

_____

_____

Critic's Voice:

_____

_____

_____

Body Connection:

_____

_____

_____

Perceived Message:

_____

_____

_____

Possible Evidence For:

_____

_____

_____

Evidence Against:

_____

_____

_____

New Learning:

_____

_____

_____

Rewriting the Script:

_____

_____

_____

Impact I Want to Have in the World Today:

_____

_____

_____

Gratitude:

_____

_____

_____

The inner critic is the voice of shame, blame, belittlement, aversion, and contempt. To many of us, it is so familiar that it seems almost hardwired into our hearts.

~Christina Feldman~

My Intention:

_____

_____

_____

Affirmation(s):

_____

_____

_____

Critic's Voice:

_____

_____

_____

Body Connection:

_____

_____

_____

Perceived Message:

_____

_____

_____

Possible Evidence For:

_____

_____

_____

Evidence Against:

_____

_____

_____

New Learning:

_____

_____

_____

Rewriting the Script:

_____

_____

_____

Impact I Want to Have in the World Today:

_____

_____

_____

Gratitude:

_____

_____

_____

*Old defense mechanisms
that are no longer needed for your survival
must be surrendered.*

~Paul Ferrini~

My Intention:

_____

_____

_____

Affirmation(s):

_____

_____

_____

Critic's Voice:

_____

_____

_____

Body Connection:

_____

_____

_____

Perceived Message:

_____

_____

_____

Possible Evidence For:

_____

_____

_____

Evidence Against:

_____

_____

_____

New Learning:

_____

_____

_____

Rewriting the Script:

_____

_____

_____

Impact I Want to Have in the World Today:

_____

_____

_____

Gratitude:

_____

_____

_____

Forgiveness of myself and others released me from the past. Forgiveness is the answer to almost every problem. Forgiveness is a gift to myself. I forgive, and I set myself free.

~Louise Hay~

My Intention:

_____

_____

_____

Affirmation(s):

_____

_____

_____

Critic's Voice:

_____

_____

_____

Body Connection:

_____

_____

_____

Perceived Message:

_____

_____

_____

Possible Evidence For:

_____

_____

_____

Evidence Against:

_____

_____

_____

New Learning:

_____

_____

_____

Rewriting the Script:

_____

_____

_____

Impact I Want to Have in the World Today:

_____

_____

_____

Gratitude:

_____

_____

_____

*Exercising patience prevents you from making
emotional decisions. Delay your actions,
deal with the emotions, then deliver a well
thought out solution that benefits you.*

~Roney McIntyre Jr~

My Intention:

_____

_____

_____

Affirmation(s):

_____

_____

_____

Critic's Voice:

_____

_____

_____

Body Connection:

_____

_____

_____

Perceived Message:

_____

_____

_____

Possible Evidence For:

_____

_____

_____

Evidence Against:

_____

_____

_____

New Learning:

_____

_____

_____

Rewriting the Script:

_____

_____

_____

Impact I Want to Have in the World Today:

_____

_____

_____

Gratitude:

_____

_____

_____

Fearlessness is like a muscle. I know from my own life that the more I exercise it the more natural it becomes to not let my fears run me.

~Arianna Huffington~

My Intention:

_____

_____

_____

Affirmation(s):

_____

_____

_____

Critic's Voice:

_____

_____

_____

Body Connection:

_____

_____

_____

Perceived Message:

_____

_____

_____

Possible Evidence For:

_____

_____

_____

Evidence Against:

_____

_____

_____

New Learning:

_____

_____

_____

Rewriting the Script:

_____

_____

_____

Impact I Want to Have in the World Today:

_____

_____

_____

Gratitude:

_____

_____

_____

*Watch out for the joy-stealers: gossip,
criticism, complaining, faultfinding, and
a negative, judgmental attitude.*

~Joyce Meyer~

My Intention:

_____

_____

_____

Affirmation(s):

_____

_____

_____

Critic's Voice:

_____

_____

_____

Body Connection:

_____

_____

_____

Perceived Message:

_____

_____

_____

Possible Evidence For:

_____

_____

_____

Evidence Against:

_____

_____

_____

New Learning:

_____

_____

_____

Rewriting the Script:

_____

_____

_____

Impact I Want to Have in the World Today:

_____

_____

_____

Gratitude:

_____

_____

_____

To avoid criticism, do nothing, say
nothing, and be nothing.

~Elbert Hubbard~

My Intention:

_____

_____

_____

Affirmation(s):

_____

_____

_____

Critic's Voice:

_____

_____

_____

Body Connection:

_____

_____

_____

Perceived Message:

_____

_____

_____

Possible Evidence For:

_____

_____

_____

Evidence Against:

_____

_____

_____

New Learning:

_____

_____

_____

Rewriting the Script:

_____

_____

_____

Impact I Want to Have in the World Today:

_____

_____

_____

Gratitude:

_____

_____

_____

You are responsible for what you believe,
even if you choose to believe what others tell you.

~Paul Ferrini~

My Intention:

_____

_____

_____

Affirmation(s):

_____

_____

_____

Critic's Voice:

_____

_____

_____

Body Connection:

_____

_____

_____

Perceived Message:

_____

_____

_____

Possible Evidence For:

_____

_____

_____

Evidence Against:

_____

_____

_____

New Learning:

_____

_____

_____

Rewriting the Script:

_____

_____

_____

Impact I Want to Have in the World Today:

_____

_____

_____

Gratitude:

_____

_____

_____

For some reason if we hear 100 praises and one criticism, we focus on that one hurtful thing.

~Carmen Electra~

My Intention:

_____

_____

_____

Affirmation(s):

_____

_____

_____

Critic's Voice:

_____

_____

_____

Body Connection:

_____

_____

_____

Perceived Message:

_____

_____

_____

Possible Evidence For:

_____

_____

_____

Evidence Against:

_____

_____

_____

New Learning:

_____

_____

_____

Rewriting the Script:

_____

_____

_____

Impact I Want to Have in the World Today:

_____

_____

_____

Gratitude:

_____

_____

_____

Life is 10% what happens to you
and 90% how you react to it.

~Charles R. Swindoll~

My Intention:

_____

_____

_____

Affirmation(s):

_____

_____

_____

Critic's Voice:

_____

_____

_____

Body Connection:

_____

_____

_____

Perceived Message:

_____

_____

_____

Possible Evidence For:

_____

_____

_____

Evidence Against:

_____

_____

_____

New Learning:

_____

_____

_____

Rewriting the Script:

_____

_____

_____

Impact I Want to Have in the World Today:

_____

_____

_____

Gratitude:

_____

_____

_____

Only I can change my life. No one can do it for me.

~Carol Burnett~

My Intention:

_____

_____

_____

Affirmation(s):

_____

_____

_____

Critic's Voice:

_____

_____

_____

Body Connection:

_____

_____

_____

Perceived Message:

_____

_____

_____

Possible Evidence For:

_____

_____

_____

Evidence Against:

_____

_____

_____

New Learning:

_____

_____

_____

Rewriting the Script:

_____

_____

_____

Impact I Want to Have in the World Today:

_____

_____

_____

Gratitude:

_____

_____

_____

*With the new day comes new
strength and new thoughts.*

~Eleanor Roosevelt~

My Intention:

_____

_____

_____

Affirmation(s):

_____

_____

_____

Critic's Voice:

_____

_____

_____

Body Connection:

_____

_____

_____

Perceived Message:

_____

_____

_____

Possible Evidence For:

_____

_____

_____

Evidence Against:

_____

_____

_____

New Learning:

_____

_____

_____

Rewriting the Script:

_____

_____

_____

Impact I Want to Have in the World Today:

_____

_____

_____

Gratitude:

_____

_____

_____

It always seems impossible until it's done.

~Nelson Mandela~

My Intention:

_____

_____

_____

Affirmation(s):

_____

_____

_____

Critic's Voice:

_____

_____

_____

Body Connection:

_____

_____

_____

Perceived Message:

_____

_____

_____

Possible Evidence For:

_____

_____

_____

Evidence Against:

_____

_____

_____

New Learning:

_____

_____

_____

Rewriting the Script:

_____

_____

_____

Impact I Want to Have in the World Today:

_____

_____

_____

Gratitude:

_____

_____

_____

*It does not matter how slowly you
go as long as you do not stop.*

~Confucius~

My Intention:

_____

_____

_____

Affirmation(s):

_____

_____

_____

Critic's Voice:

_____

_____

_____

Body Connection:

_____

_____

_____

Perceived Message:

_____

_____

_____

Possible Evidence For:

_____

_____

_____

Evidence Against:

_____

_____

_____

New Learning:

_____

_____

_____

Rewriting the Script:

_____

_____

_____

Impact I Want to Have in the World Today:

_____

_____

_____

Gratitude:

_____

_____

_____

*Failure will never overtake me if my
determination to succeed is strong enough.*

~ Og Mandino ~

My Intention:

_____

_____

_____

Affirmation(s):

_____

_____

_____

Critic's Voice:

_____

_____

_____

Body Connection:

_____

_____

_____

Perceived Message:

_____

_____

_____

Possible Evidence For:

_____

_____

_____

Evidence Against:

_____

_____

_____

New Learning:

_____

_____

_____

Rewriting the Script:

_____

_____

_____

Impact I Want to Have in the World Today:

_____

_____

_____

Gratitude:

_____

_____

_____

*A journey of a thousand miles must
begin with a single step.*

~Lao Tzu~

My Intention:

_____

_____

_____

Affirmation(s):

_____

_____

_____

Critic's Voice:

_____

_____

_____

Body Connection:

_____

_____

_____

Perceived Message:

_____

_____

_____

Possible Evidence For:

_____

_____

_____

Evidence Against:

_____

_____

_____

New Learning:

_____

_____

_____

Rewriting the Script:

_____

_____

_____

Impact I Want to Have in the World Today:

_____

_____

_____

Gratitude:

_____

_____

_____

*Setting goals is the first step in turning
the invisible into the visible.*

~Tony Robbins~

My Intention:

_____

_____

_____

Affirmation(s):

_____

_____

_____

Critic's Voice:

_____

_____

_____

Body Connection:

_____

_____

_____

Perceived Message:

_____

_____

_____

Possible Evidence For:

_____

_____

_____

Evidence Against:

_____

_____

_____

New Learning:

_____

_____

_____

Rewriting the Script:

_____

_____

_____

Impact I Want to Have in the World Today:

_____

_____

_____

Gratitude:

_____

_____

_____

If you can dream it, you can do it.

~Walt Disney~

My Intention:

_____

_____

_____

Affirmation(s):

_____

_____

_____

Critic's Voice:

_____

_____

_____

Body Connection:

_____

_____

_____

Perceived Message:

_____

_____

_____

Possible Evidence For:

_____

_____

_____

Evidence Against:

_____

_____

_____

New Learning:

_____

_____

_____

Rewriting the Script:

_____

_____

_____

Impact I Want to Have in the World Today:

_____

_____

_____

Gratitude:

_____

_____

_____

There is only one corner of the universe you can be certain of improving, and that's your own self.

~Aldous Huxley~

My Intention:

_____

_____

_____

Affirmation(s):

_____

_____

_____

Critic's Voice:

_____

_____

_____

Body Connection:

_____

_____

_____

Perceived Message:

_____

_____

_____

Possible Evidence For:

_____

_____

_____

Evidence Against:

_____

_____

_____

New Learning:

_____

_____

_____

Rewriting the Script:

_____

_____

_____

Impact I Want to Have in the World Today:

_____

_____

_____

Gratitude:

_____

_____

_____

Never, never, never give up.

~Winston Churchill~

My Intention:

_____

_____

_____

Affirmation(s):

_____

_____

_____

Critic's Voice:

_____

_____

_____

Body Connection:

_____

_____

_____

Perceived Message:

_____

_____

_____

Possible Evidence For:

_____

_____

_____

Evidence Against:

_____

_____

_____

New Learning:

_____

_____

_____

Rewriting the Script:

_____

_____

_____

Impact I Want to Have in the World Today:

_____

_____

_____

Gratitude:

_____

_____

_____

Be kind whenever possible. It is always possible.

~Dalai Lama~

My Intention:

_____

_____

_____

Affirmation(s):

_____

_____

_____

Critic's Voice:

_____

_____

_____

Body Connection:

_____

_____

_____

Perceived Message:

_____

_____

_____

Possible Evidence For:

_____

_____

_____

Evidence Against:

_____

_____

_____

New Learning:

_____

_____

_____

Rewriting the Script:

_____

_____

_____

Impact I Want to Have in the World Today:

_____

_____

_____

Gratitude:

_____

_____

_____

If you're going through hell, keep going.

~Winston Churchill~

My Intention:

_____

_____

_____

Affirmation(s):

_____

_____

_____

Critic's Voice:

_____

_____

_____

Body Connection:

_____

_____

_____

Perceived Message:

_____

_____

_____

Possible Evidence For:

_____

_____

_____

Evidence Against:

_____

_____

_____

New Learning:

_____

_____

_____

Rewriting the Script:

_____

_____

_____

Impact I Want to Have in the World Today:

_____

_____

_____

Gratitude:

_____

_____

_____

Do you want to know who you are? Don't ask. Act!
Action will delineate and define you.

~Thomas Jefferson~

My Intention:

_____

_____

_____

Affirmation(s):

_____

_____

_____

Critic's Voice:

_____

_____

_____

Body Connection:

_____

_____

_____

Perceived Message:

_____

_____

_____

Possible Evidence For:

_____

_____

_____

Evidence Against:

_____

_____

_____

New Learning:

_____

_____

_____

Rewriting the Script:

_____

_____

_____

Impact I Want to Have in the World Today:

_____

_____

_____

Gratitude:

_____

_____

_____

Be miserable. Or motivate yourself. Whatever has to be done, it's always your choice.

~Wayne Dyer~

My Intention:

_____

_____

_____

Affirmation(s):

_____

_____

_____

Critic's Voice:

_____

_____

_____

Body Connection:

_____

_____

_____

Perceived Message:

_____

_____

_____

Possible Evidence For:

_____

_____

_____

Evidence Against:

_____

_____

_____

New Learning:

_____

_____

_____

Rewriting the Script:

_____

_____

_____

Impact I Want to Have in the World Today:

_____

_____

_____

Gratitude:

_____

_____

_____

It is never too late to be what you might have been.

~George Eliot~

My Intention:

_____

_____

_____

Affirmation(s):

_____

_____

_____

Critic's Voice:

_____

_____

Body Connection:

_____

_____

Perceived Message:

_____

_____

_____

Possible Evidence For:

_____

_____

_____

Evidence Against:

_____

_____

_____

New Learning:

_____

_____

_____

Rewriting the Script:

_____

_____

_____

Impact I Want to Have in the World Today:

_____

_____

_____

Gratitude:

_____

_____

_____

*I know where I'm going and I know the truth, and
I don't have to be what you want me to be.
I'm free to be what I want.*

~Muhammad Ali ~

My Intention:

_____

_____

_____

Affirmation(s):

_____

_____

_____

Critic's Voice:

_____

_____

_____

Body Connection:

_____

_____

_____

Perceived Message:

_____

_____

_____

Possible Evidence For:

_____

_____

_____

Evidence Against:

_____

_____

_____

New Learning:

_____

_____

_____

Rewriting the Script:

_____

_____

_____

Impact I Want to Have in the World Today:

_____

_____

_____

Gratitude:

_____

_____

_____

Deserve your dream.

~Octavio Paz~

My Intention:

_____

_____

_____

Affirmation(s):

_____

_____

_____

Critic's Voice:

_____

_____

_____

Body Connection:

_____

_____

_____

Perceived Message:

_____

_____

_____

Possible Evidence For:

_____

_____

_____

Evidence Against:

_____

_____

_____

New Learning:

_____

_____

_____

Rewriting the Script:

_____

_____

_____

Impact I Want to Have in the World Today:

_____

_____

_____

Gratitude:

_____

_____

_____

I am not a has-been. I am a will be.

~Lauren Bacall~

My Intention:

_____

_____

_____

Affirmation(s):

_____

_____

_____

Critic's Voice:

_____

_____

_____

Body Connection:

_____

_____

_____

Perceived Message:

_____

_____

_____

Possible Evidence For:

_____

_____

_____

Evidence Against:

_____

_____

_____

New Learning:

_____

_____

_____

Rewriting the Script:

_____

_____

_____

Impact I Want to Have in the World Today:

_____

_____

_____

Gratitude:

_____

_____

_____

I am the maker of my own fortune.

~Tecumseh~

My Intention:

_____

_____

_____

Affirmation(s):

_____

_____

_____

Critic's Voice:

_____

_____

_____

Body Connection:

_____

_____

_____

Perceived Message:

_____

_____

_____

Possible Evidence For:

_____

_____

_____

Evidence Against:

_____

_____

_____

New Learning:

_____

_____

_____

Rewriting the Script:

_____

_____

_____

Impact I Want to Have in the World Today:

_____

_____

_____

Gratitude:

_____

_____

_____

We must let go of the life we have planned, so as to accept the one that is waiting for us.

~Joseph Campbell~

My Intention:

_____

_____

_____

Affirmation(s):

_____

_____

_____

Critic's Voice:

_____

_____

_____

Body Connection:

_____

_____

_____

Perceived Message:

_____

_____

_____

Possible Evidence For:

_____

_____

_____

Evidence Against:

_____

_____

_____

New Learning:

_____

_____

_____

Rewriting the Script:

_____

_____

_____

Impact I Want to Have in the World Today:

_____

_____

_____

Gratitude:

_____

_____

_____

*I can't change the direction of the wind, but I can
adjust my sails to always reach my destination.*

~Jimmy Dean~

My Intention:

_____

_____

_____

Affirmation(s):

_____

_____

_____

Critic's Voice:

_____

_____

_____

Body Connection:

_____

_____

_____

Perceived Message:

_____

_____

_____

Possible Evidence For:

_____

_____

_____

Evidence Against:

_____

_____

_____

New Learning:

_____

_____

_____

Rewriting the Script:

_____

_____

_____

Impact I Want to Have in the World Today:

_____

_____

_____

Gratitude:

_____

_____

_____

My mission in life is not merely to survive, but to thrive; and to do so with some passion, some compassion, some humor, and some style.

~Maya Angelou~

My Intention:

_____

_____

_____

Affirmation(s):

_____

_____

_____

Critic's Voice:

_____

_____

_____

Body Connection:

_____

_____

_____

Perceived Message:

_____

_____

_____

Possible Evidence For:

_____

_____

_____

Evidence Against:

_____

_____

_____

New Learning:

_____

_____

_____

Rewriting the Script:

_____

_____

_____

Impact I Want to Have in the World Today:

_____

_____

_____

Gratitude:

_____

_____

_____

Happiness is not something you postpone for the future; it is something you design for the present.

~Jim Rohn~

My Intention:

_____

_____

_____

Affirmation(s):

_____

_____

_____

Critic's Voice:

_____

_____

_____

Body Connection:

_____

_____

_____

Perceived Message:

_____

_____

_____

Possible Evidence For:

_____

_____

_____

Evidence Against:

_____

_____

_____

New Learning:

_____

_____

_____

Rewriting the Script:

_____

_____

_____

Impact I Want to Have in the World Today:

_____

_____

_____

Gratitude:

_____

_____

_____

Keep your face always toward the sunshine
– and shadows will fall behind you.

~ Walt Whitman ~

My Intention:

_____

_____

_____

Affirmation(s):

_____

_____

_____

Critic's Voice:

_____

_____

_____

Body Connection:

_____

_____

_____

Perceived Message:

_____

_____

_____

Possible Evidence For:

_____

_____

_____

Evidence Against:

_____

_____

_____

New Learning:

_____

_____

_____

Rewriting the Script:

_____

_____

_____

Impact I Want to Have in the World Today:

_____

_____

_____

Gratitude:

_____

_____

_____

Change your thoughts and you change your world.

~Norman Vincent Peale~

My Intention:

_____

_____

_____

Affirmation(s):

_____

_____

_____

Critic's Voice:

_____

_____

_____

Body Connection:

_____

_____

_____

Perceived Message:

_____

_____

_____

Possible Evidence For:

_____

_____

_____

Evidence Against:

_____

_____

_____

New Learning:

_____

_____

_____

Rewriting the Script:

_____

_____

_____

Impact I Want to Have in the World Today:

_____

_____

_____

Gratitude:

_____

_____

_____

What lies behind you and what lies in front of you,
pales in comparison to what lies inside of you.

~Ralph Waldo Emerson~

My Intention:

_____

_____

_____

Affirmation(s):

_____

_____

_____

Critic's Voice:

_____

_____

_____

Body Connection:

_____

_____

_____

Perceived Message:

_____

_____

_____

Possible Evidence For:

_____

_____

_____

Evidence Against:

_____

_____

_____

New Learning:

_____

_____

_____

Rewriting the Script:

_____

_____

_____

Impact I Want to Have in the World Today:

_____

_____

_____

Gratitude:

_____

_____

_____

We know what we are, but know
not what we may be.

~William Shakespeare~

My Intention:

_____

_____

_____

Affirmation(s):

_____

_____

_____

Critic's Voice:

_____

_____

_____

Body Connection:

_____

_____

_____

Perceived Message:

_____

_____

_____

Possible Evidence For:

_____

_____

_____

Evidence Against:

_____

_____

_____

New Learning:

_____

_____

_____

Rewriting the Script:

_____

_____

_____

Impact I Want to Have in the World Today:

_____

_____

_____

Gratitude:

_____

_____

_____

Follow your bliss and the universe will open doors where there were only walls.

~Joseph Campbell~

My Intention:

_____

_____

_____

Affirmation(s):

_____

_____

_____

Critic's Voice:

_____

_____

_____

Body Connection:

_____

_____

_____

Perceived Message:

_____

_____

_____

Possible Evidence For:

_____

_____

_____

Evidence Against:

_____

_____

_____

New Learning:

_____

_____

_____

Rewriting the Script:

_____

_____

_____

Impact I Want to Have in the World Today:

_____

_____

_____

Gratitude:

_____

_____

_____

*Everyone has inside of him a piece of good news.
The good news is that you don't know how great
you can be! How much you can love! What you
can accomplish! And what your potential is!*

~Anne Frank~

My Intention:

_____

_____

_____

Affirmation(s):

_____

_____

_____

Critic's Voice:

_____

_____

_____

Body Connection:

_____

_____

_____

Perceived Message:

_____

_____

_____

Possible Evidence For:

_____

_____

_____

Evidence Against:

_____

_____

_____

New Learning:

_____

_____

_____

Rewriting the Script:

_____

_____

_____

Impact I Want to Have in the World Today:

_____

_____

_____

Gratitude:

_____

_____

_____

If we did all the things we are capable of,
we would literally astound ourselves.

~Thomas A. Edison~

My Intention:

_____

_____

_____

Affirmation(s):

_____

_____

_____

Critic's Voice:

_____

_____

_____

Body Connection:

_____

_____

_____

Perceived Message:

_____

_____

_____

Possible Evidence For:

_____

_____

_____

Evidence Against:

_____

_____

_____

New Learning:

_____

_____

_____

Rewriting the Script:

_____

_____

_____

Impact I Want to Have in the World Today:

_____

_____

_____

Gratitude:

_____

_____

_____

What we achieve inwardly will change outer reality.

~Plutarch~

My Intention:

_____

_____

_____

Affirmation(s):

_____

_____

_____

Critic's Voice:

_____

_____

_____

Body Connection:

_____

_____

_____

Perceived Message:

_____

_____

_____

Possible Evidence For:

_____

_____

_____

Evidence Against:

_____

_____

_____

New Learning:

_____

_____

_____

Rewriting the Script:

_____

_____

_____

Impact I Want to Have in the World Today:

_____

_____

_____

Gratitude:

_____

_____

_____

Once we believe in ourselves, we can risk curiosity, wonder, spontaneous delight, or any experience that reveals the human spirit.

~e. e. cummings~

My Intention:

_____

_____

_____

Affirmation(s):

_____

_____

_____

Critic's Voice:

_____

_____

_____

Body Connection:

_____

_____

_____

Perceived Message:

_____

_____

_____

Possible Evidence For:

_____

_____

_____

Evidence Against:

_____

_____

_____

New Learning:

_____

_____

_____

Rewriting the Script:

_____

_____

_____

Impact I Want to Have in the World Today:

_____

_____

_____

Gratitude:

_____

_____

_____

The only journey is the one within.

~Rainer Maria Rilke~

My Intention:

_____

_____

_____

Affirmation(s):

_____

_____

_____

Critic's Voice:

_____

_____

_____

Body Connection:

_____

_____

_____

Perceived Message:

_____

_____

_____

Possible Evidence For:

_____

_____

_____

Evidence Against:

_____

_____

_____

New Learning:

_____

_____

_____

Rewriting the Script:

_____

_____

_____

Impact I Want to Have in the World Today:

_____

_____

_____

Gratitude:

_____

_____

_____

The best way out is always through.

~Robert Frost~

My Intention:

_____

_____

_____

Affirmation(s):

_____

_____

_____

Critic's Voice:

_____

_____

_____

Body Connection:

_____

_____

Perceived Message:

_____

_____

_____

Possible Evidence For:

_____

_____

_____

Evidence Against:

_____

_____

_____

New Learning:

_____

_____

_____

Rewriting the Script:

_____

_____

_____

Impact I Want to Have in the World Today:

_____

_____

_____

Gratitude:

_____

_____

_____

*The most authentic thing about us is our capacity
to create, to overcome, to endure, to transform,
to love and to be greater than our suffering.*

~Ben Okri~

My Intention:

_____

_____

_____

Affirmation(s):

_____

_____

_____

Critic's Voice:

_____

_____

_____

Body Connection:

_____

_____

_____

Perceived Message:

_____

_____

_____

Possible Evidence For:

_____

_____

_____

Evidence Against:

_____

_____

_____

New Learning:

_____

_____

_____

Rewriting the Script:

_____

_____

_____

Impact I Want to Have in the World Today:

_____

_____

_____

Gratitude:

_____

_____

_____

Vitality shows in not only the ability to persist but the ability to start over.

~F. Scott Fitzgerald~

My Intention:

_____

_____

_____

Affirmation(s):

_____

_____

_____

Critic's Voice:

_____

_____

_____

Body Connection:

_____

_____

_____

Perceived Message:

_____

_____

_____

Possible Evidence For:

_____

_____

_____

Evidence Against:

_____

_____

_____

New Learning:

_____

_____

_____

Rewriting the Script:

_____

_____

_____

Impact I Want to Have in the World Today:

_____

_____

_____

Gratitude:

_____

_____

_____

You change your life by changing your heart.

~Max Lucado~

My Intention:

_____

_____

_____

Affirmation(s):

_____

_____

_____

Critic's Voice:

_____

_____

_____

Body Connection:

_____

_____

_____

Perceived Message:

_____

_____

_____

Possible Evidence For:

_____

_____

_____

Evidence Against:

_____

_____

_____

New Learning:

_____

_____

_____

Rewriting the Script:

_____

_____

_____

Impact I Want to Have in the World Today:

_____

_____

_____

Gratitude:

_____

_____

_____

Everything you want is out there waiting for you to ask. Everything you want also wants you. But you have to take action to get it.

~Jules Renard~

My Intention:

_____

_____

_____

Affirmation(s):

_____

_____

_____

Critic's Voice:

_____

_____

_____

Body Connection:

_____

_____

_____

Perceived Message:

_____

_____

_____

Possible Evidence For:

_____

_____

_____

Evidence Against:

_____

_____

_____

New Learning:

_____

_____

_____

Rewriting the Script:

_____

_____

_____

Impact I Want to Have in the World Today:

_____

_____

_____

Gratitude:

_____

_____

_____

Live your beliefs and you can turn the world around.

~Henry David Thoreau~

My Intention:

_____

_____

_____

Affirmation(s):

_____

_____

_____

Critic's Voice:

_____

_____

_____

Body Connection:

_____

_____

_____

Perceived Message:

_____

_____

_____

Possible Evidence For:

_____

_____

_____

Evidence Against:

_____

_____

_____

New Learning:

_____

_____

_____

Rewriting the Script:

_____

_____

_____

Impact I Want to Have in the World Today:

_____

_____

_____

Gratitude:

_____

_____

_____

*Most of us have far more courage than
we ever dreamed we possessed.*

~Dale Carnegie~

My Intention:

_____

_____

_____

Affirmation(s):

_____

_____

_____

Critic's Voice:

_____

_____

_____

Body Connection:

_____

_____

_____

Perceived Message:

_____

_____

_____

Possible Evidence For:

_____

_____

_____

Evidence Against:

_____

_____

_____

New Learning:

_____

_____

_____

Rewriting the Script:

_____

_____

_____

Impact I Want to Have in the World Today:

_____

_____

_____

Gratitude:

_____

_____

_____

We must let go of the life we have planned, so as to accept the one that is waiting for us.

~Joseph Campbell~

My Intention:

_____

_____

_____

Affirmation(s):

_____

_____

_____

Critic's Voice:

_____

_____

_____

Body Connection:

_____

_____

_____

Perceived Message:

_____

_____

_____

Possible Evidence For:

_____

_____

_____

Evidence Against:

_____

_____

_____

New Learning:

_____

_____

_____

Rewriting the Script:

_____

_____

_____

Impact I Want to Have in the World Today:

_____

_____

_____

Gratitude:

_____

_____

_____

*Life isn't about finding yourself. Life
is about creating yourself.*

~George Bernard Shaw~

My Intention:

_____

_____

_____

Affirmation(s):

_____

_____

_____

Critic's Voice:

_____

_____

_____

Body Connection:

_____

_____

_____

Perceived Message:

_____

_____

_____

Possible Evidence For:

_____

_____

_____

Evidence Against:

_____

_____

_____

New Learning:

_____

_____

_____

Rewriting the Script:

_____

_____

_____

Impact I Want to Have in the World Today:

_____

_____

_____

Gratitude:

_____

_____

_____

The unexamined life is not worth living.

~Socrates~

My Intention:

_____

_____

_____

Affirmation(s):

_____

_____

_____

Critic's Voice:

_____

_____

_____

Body Connection:

_____

_____

_____

Perceived Message:

_____

_____

_____

Possible Evidence For:

_____

_____

_____

Evidence Against:

_____

_____

_____

New Learning:

_____

_____

_____

Rewriting the Script:

_____

_____

_____

Impact I Want to Have in the World Today:

_____

_____

_____

Gratitude:

_____

_____

_____

Live life to the fullest, and focus on the positive.

~Matt Cameron~

My Intention:

_____

_____

_____

Affirmation(s):

_____

_____

_____

Critic's Voice:

_____

_____

_____

Body Connection:

_____

_____

_____

Perceived Message:

_____

_____

_____

Possible Evidence For:

_____

_____

_____

Evidence Against:

_____

_____

_____

New Learning:

_____

_____

_____

Rewriting the Script:

_____

_____

_____

Impact I Want to Have in the World Today:

_____

_____

_____

Gratitude:

_____

_____

_____

The good life is one inspired by love
and guided by knowledge.

~Bertrand Russell~

My Intention:

_____

_____

_____

Affirmation(s):

_____

_____

_____

Critic's Voice:

_____

_____

_____

Body Connection:

_____

_____

_____

Perceived Message:

_____

_____

_____

Possible Evidence For:

_____

_____

_____

Evidence Against:

_____

_____

_____

New Learning:

_____

_____

_____

Rewriting the Script:

_____

_____

_____

Impact I Want to Have in the World Today:

_____

_____

_____

Gratitude:

_____

_____

_____

*Life is really simple, but we insist
on making it complicated.*

~Confucius~

My Intention:

_____

_____

_____

Affirmation(s):

_____

_____

_____

Critic's Voice:

_____

_____

_____

Body Connection:

_____

_____

_____

Perceived Message:

_____

_____

_____

Possible Evidence For:

_____

_____

_____

Evidence Against:

_____

_____

_____

New Learning:

_____

_____

_____

Rewriting the Script:

_____

_____

_____

Impact I Want to Have in the World Today:

_____

_____

_____

Gratitude:

_____

_____

_____

You're going to go through tough times - that's life. But I say, 'Nothing happens to you, it happens for you. See the positive in negative events."

~Joel Osteen~

My Intention:

_____

_____

_____

Affirmation(s):

_____

_____

_____

Critic's Voice:

_____

_____

_____

Body Connection:

_____

_____

_____

Perceived Message:

_____

_____

_____

Possible Evidence For:

_____

_____

_____

Evidence Against:

_____

_____

_____

New Learning:

_____

_____

_____

Rewriting the Script:

_____

_____

_____

Impact I Want to Have in the World Today:

_____

_____

_____

Gratitude:

_____

_____

_____

*Life was always a matter of waiting
for the right moment to act.*

~Paulo Coelho~

My Intention:

_____

_____

_____

Affirmation(s):

_____

_____

_____

Critic's Voice:

_____

_____

_____

Body Connection:

_____

_____

_____

Perceived Message:

_____

_____

_____

Possible Evidence For:

_____

_____

_____

Evidence Against:

_____

_____

_____

New Learning:

_____

_____

_____

Rewriting the Script:

_____

_____

_____

Impact I Want to Have in the World Today:

_____

_____

_____

Gratitude:

_____

_____

_____

I used to think that the worst thing in life was to end up alone. It's not. The worst thing in life is to end up with people who make you feel alone.

~Robin Williams~

My Intention:

_____

_____

_____

Affirmation(s):

_____

_____

_____

Critic's Voice:

_____

_____

_____

Body Connection:

_____

_____

_____

Perceived Message:

_____

_____

_____

Possible Evidence For:

_____

_____

_____

Evidence Against:

_____

_____

_____

New Learning:

_____

_____

_____

Rewriting the Script:

_____

_____

_____

Impact I Want to Have in the World Today:

_____

_____

_____

Gratitude:

_____

_____

_____

If you have no confidence in self, you are
twice defeated in the race of life.

~Marcus Garvey~

My Intention:

_____

_____

_____

Affirmation(s):

_____

_____

_____

Critic's Voice:

_____

_____

_____

Body Connection:

_____

_____

_____

Perceived Message:

_____

_____

_____

Possible Evidence For:

_____

_____

_____

Evidence Against:

_____

_____

_____

New Learning:

_____

_____

_____

Rewriting the Script:

_____

_____

_____

Impact I Want to Have in the World Today:

_____

_____

_____

Gratitude:

_____

_____

_____

*Hold fast to dreams, for if dreams die, life
is a broken-winged bird that cannot fly.*

~Langston Hughes~

My Intention:

_____

_____

_____

Affirmation(s):

_____

_____

_____

Critic's Voice:

_____

_____

_____

Body Connection:

_____

_____

_____

Perceived Message:

_____

_____

_____

Possible Evidence For:

_____

_____

_____

Evidence Against:

_____

_____

_____

New Learning:

_____

_____

_____

Rewriting the Script:

_____

_____

_____

Impact I Want to Have in the World Today:

_____

_____

_____

Gratitude:

_____

_____

_____

*Our prime purpose in this life is to help others. And
if you can't help them, at least don't hurt them.*

~Dalai Lama~

My Intention:

_____

_____

_____

Affirmation(s):

_____

_____

_____

Critic's Voice:

_____

_____

_____

Body Connection:

_____

_____

_____

Perceived Message:

_____

_____

_____

Possible Evidence For:

_____

_____

_____

Evidence Against:

_____

_____

_____

New Learning:

_____

_____

_____

Rewriting the Script:

_____

_____

_____

Impact I Want to Have in the World Today:

_____

_____

_____

Gratitude:

_____

_____

_____

Trust yourself. Create the kind of self that you will be happy to live with all your life. Make the most of yourself by fanning the tiny, inner sparks of possibility into flames of achievement.

~Golda Meir~

My Intention:

_____

_____

_____

Affirmation(s):

_____

_____

_____

Critic's Voice:

_____

_____

_____

Body Connection:

_____

_____

_____

Perceived Message:

_____

_____

_____

Possible Evidence For:

_____

_____

_____

Evidence Against:

_____

_____

_____

New Learning:

_____

_____

_____

Rewriting the Script:

_____

_____

_____

Impact I Want to Have in the World Today:

_____

_____

_____

Gratitude:

_____

_____

_____

*Life is a mirror and will reflect back to
the thinker what he thinks into it.*

~Ernest Holmes~

My Intention:

_____

_____

_____

Affirmation(s):

_____

_____

_____

Critic's Voice:

_____

_____

_____

Body Connection:

_____

_____

_____

Perceived Message:

_____

_____

_____

Possible Evidence For:

_____

_____

_____

Evidence Against:

_____

_____

_____

New Learning:

_____

_____

_____

Rewriting the Script:

_____

_____

_____

Impact I Want to Have in the World Today:

_____

_____

_____

Gratitude:

_____

_____

_____

Open your eyes, look within. Are you satisfied with the life you're living?

~Bob Marley~

My Intention:

_____

_____

_____

Affirmation(s):

_____

_____

_____

Critic's Voice:

_____

_____

_____

Body Connection:

_____

_____

_____

Perceived Message:

_____

_____

_____

Possible Evidence For:

_____

_____

_____

Evidence Against:

_____

_____

_____

New Learning:

_____

_____

_____

Rewriting the Script:

_____

_____

_____

Impact I Want to Have in the World Today:

_____

_____

_____

Gratitude:

_____

_____

_____

You cannot have a positive life and a negative mind.

~Joyce Meyer~

My Intention:

_____

_____

_____

Affirmation(s):

_____

_____

_____

Critic's Voice:

_____

_____

_____

Body Connection:

_____

_____

_____

Perceived Message:

_____

_____

_____

Possible Evidence For:

_____

_____

_____

Evidence Against:

_____

_____

_____

New Learning:

_____

_____

_____

Rewriting the Script:

_____

_____

_____

Impact I Want to Have in the World Today:

_____

_____

_____

Gratitude:

_____

_____

_____

Life is not a solo act. It's a huge collaboration, and we all need to assemble around us the people who care about us and support us in times of strife.

~Tim Gunn~

My Intention:

_____

_____

_____

Affirmation(s):

_____

_____

_____

Critic's Voice:

_____

_____

_____

Body Connection:

_____

_____

_____

Perceived Message:

_____

_____

_____

Possible Evidence For:

_____

_____

_____

Evidence Against:

_____

_____

_____

New Learning:

_____

_____

_____

Rewriting the Script:

_____

_____

_____

Impact I Want to Have in the World Today:

_____

_____

_____

Gratitude:

_____

_____

_____

Life is a series of waves to be
embraced and overcome.

~Danny Meyer~

My Intention:

_____

_____

_____

Affirmation(s):

_____

_____

_____

Critic's Voice:

_____

_____

_____

Body Connection:

_____

_____

_____

Perceived Message:

_____

_____

_____

Possible Evidence For:

_____

_____

_____

Evidence Against:

_____

_____

_____

New Learning:

_____

_____

_____

Rewriting the Script:

_____

_____

_____

Impact I Want to Have in the World Today:

_____

_____

_____

Gratitude:

_____

_____

_____

There are two primary choices in life: to accept conditions as they exist, or accept the responsibility for changing them.

~Denis Waitley~

My Intention:

_____

_____

_____

Affirmation(s):

_____

_____

_____

Critic's Voice:

_____

_____

_____

Body Connection:

_____

_____

_____

Perceived Message:

_____

_____

_____

Possible Evidence For:

_____

_____

_____

Evidence Against:

_____

_____

_____

New Learning:

_____

_____

_____

Rewriting the Script:

_____

_____

_____

Impact I Want to Have in the World Today:

_____

_____

_____

Gratitude:

_____

_____

_____

Every thought that you have impacts you

BY shifting from a thought that weakens to one that strengthens, you raise your energy vibration and strengthen yourself and the immediate energy field.

~Wayne Dyer~

My Intention:

_____

_____

_____

Affirmation(s):

_____

_____

_____

Critic's Voice:

_____

_____

_____

Body Connection:

_____

_____

_____

Perceived Message:

_____

_____

_____

Possible Evidence For:

_____

_____

_____

Evidence Against:

_____

_____

_____

New Learning:

_____

_____

_____

Rewriting the Script:

_____

_____

_____

Impact I Want to Have in the World Today:

_____

_____

_____

Gratitude:

_____

_____

_____

Human beings, we have dark sides; we have dark issues in our lives. To progress anywhere in life, you have to face your demons.

~John Noble~

My Intention:

_____

_____

_____

Affirmation(s):

_____

_____

_____

Critic's Voice:

_____

_____

_____

Body Connection:

_____

_____

_____

Perceived Message:

_____

_____

_____

Possible Evidence For:

_____

_____

_____

Evidence Against:

_____

_____

_____

New Learning:

_____

_____

_____

Rewriting the Script:

_____

_____

_____

Impact I Want to Have in the World Today:

_____

_____

_____

Gratitude:

_____

_____

_____

Nothing in life is to be feared, it is only to be understood. Now is the time to understand more, so that we may fear less.

~Marie Curie~

My Intention:

_____

_____

_____

Affirmation(s):

_____

_____

_____

Critic's Voice:

_____

_____

_____

Body Connection:

_____

_____

_____

Perceived Message:

_____

_____

_____

Possible Evidence For:

_____

_____

_____

Evidence Against:

_____

_____

_____

New Learning:

_____

_____

_____

Rewriting the Script:

_____

_____

_____

Impact I Want to Have in the World Today:

_____

_____

_____

Gratitude:

_____

_____

_____

*The curious paradox is that when I accept
myself just as I am, then I can change.*

~Carl Rogers~

My Intention:

_____

_____

_____

Affirmation(s):

_____

_____

_____

Critic's Voice:

_____

_____

_____

Body Connection:

_____

_____

_____

Perceived Message:

_____

_____

_____

Possible Evidence For:

_____

_____

_____

Evidence Against:

_____

_____

_____

New Learning:

_____

_____

_____

Rewriting the Script:

_____

_____

_____

Impact I Want to Have in the World Today:

_____

_____

_____

Gratitude:

_____

_____

_____

*Life always reveals to me what I need
to know at just the right moment.*

~Louise Hay~

My Intention:

_____

_____

_____

Affirmation(s):

_____

_____

_____

Critic's Voice:

_____

_____

_____

Body Connection:

_____

_____

_____

Perceived Message:

_____

_____

_____

Possible Evidence For:

_____

_____

_____

Evidence Against:

_____

_____

_____

New Learning:

_____

_____

_____

Rewriting the Script:

_____

_____

_____

Impact I Want to Have in the World Today:

_____

_____

_____

Gratitude:

_____

_____

_____

Your life will be so much better when you start
trying to understand and have compassion
for people who hurt you – instead of just
reacting and hurting them back.

~Bryant McGill~

My Intention:

_____

_____

_____

Affirmation(s):

_____

_____

_____

Critic's Voice:

_____

_____

_____

Body Connection:

_____

_____

_____

Perceived Message:

_____

_____

_____

Possible Evidence For:

_____

_____

_____

Evidence Against:

_____

_____

_____

New Learning:

_____

_____

_____

Rewriting the Script:

_____

_____

_____

Impact I Want to Have in the World Today:

_____

_____

_____

Gratitude:

_____

_____

_____

Stress, anxiety and depression are caused when we are living to please others.

~Paulo Coehlo~

My Intention:

_____

_____

_____

Affirmation(s):

_____

_____

_____

Critic's Voice:

_____

_____

_____

Body Connection:

_____

_____

_____

Perceived Message:

_____

_____

_____

Possible Evidence For:

_____

_____

_____

Evidence Against:

_____

_____

_____

New Learning:

_____

_____

_____

Rewriting the Script:

_____

_____

_____

Impact I Want to Have in the World Today:

_____

_____

_____

Gratitude:

_____

_____

_____

People inspire you, or they drain you - pick them wisely.

~Hans F. Hansen~

My Intention:

_____

_____

_____

Affirmation(s):

_____

_____

_____

Critic's Voice:

_____

_____

_____

Body Connection:

_____

_____

_____

Perceived Message:

_____

_____

_____

_____

Great minds discuss ideas, average ones discuss events, and small minds discuss people.

~Eleanor Roosevelt~

My Intention:

_____

_____

_____

Affirmation(s):

_____

_____

_____

Critic's Voice:

_____

_____

_____

Body Connection:

_____

_____

_____

Perceived Message:

_____

_____

_____

In our subconscious, we all know
we are playing roles.

~RuPaul~

It can be really challenging to stand up to our critic(s) and there are many emotions that accompany those exchanges. Sometimes, the words we want to say in response come easily to us. At other times, we struggle to find the language that best captures our thoughts and emotions.

Role play with a trusted ally is invaluable when it comes to honing our skills. You can set up a scenario with your role play partner that mirrors an experience you have had or you can create several scenarios that are new so that you can think on your feet.

Play them out with your friend and ask them to mirror back what they heard and felt in the scenario. Here is a time when our inner critic might take the liberty to jump in because we are actually asking for feedback. Don't allow that to shut you down. The feedback is meant to help you grow and make you stronger. Take the feedback in and grow beyond that inner critic.

A good way to let your critic know you are feeling uncomfortable is to use an "I" message. The format for that message might look like:

When people criticize me; I feel hurt.

I-messages provide feedback safely because you are avoiding put downs, judgement or assigning blame. When providing effective feedback in this way to someone about their behaviour. These are:

describing the behaviour,

the feeling the behaviour creates and

The script will be as follows:

When STATE THE BEHAVIOUR; I feel NAME THE FEELING.

It is important to note that you will not use the word "you" as that pronoun can push people's buttons when used in this way. It can be a trigger if I say:

When YOU criticized me; I felt hurt. Leave the word "you" out of it and turn it into the third person or back to you. For example:

When I was criticized; I felt hurt.

Gratitude is one of the strongest and most transformative states of being. It shifts your perspective from lack to abundance and allows you to focus on the good in your life, which in turn pulls more goodness into your reality.

~Jen Sincero~

Congratulations!

It's been a journey and you have taken many steps to get to this point. Some of the steps have been baby ones as you gathered your courage; others have been giant leaps that propelled you forward. Perhaps there were days when there were no steps because you found yourself stuck. None of that matters now. You did it!

It's time to celebrate and pat yourself on the back for the work you have put in. It has not been easy but you made it this far. Now, it is time to ask yourself what you will do next.

- Will you stop here because you have learned the lessons?

- Will you continue the journey by maintaining the daily routine?

- Will you teach others what you have learned?

There are so many possibilities and it is up to you to decide. You no longer need any critic telling you what to do and what not to do. You have the skills to make your own plan for continuing to move forward. You will set your own boundaries.

To bring closure to the process, spend a bit of time reflecting and setting one final intention. Re-visit your writing after a period of time you set for yourself and take note of the shifts you have made. Embrace them. Celebrate them. Honour them and yourself. You now have a new story!

Believe in you, stay in the moment and
continue to free yourself for possibility!

~Jackie Eldridge~

My Final Reflections:

_____
_____
_____
_____
_____
_____
_____
_____
_____
_____
_____
_____
_____
_____

My Intention(s) to move forward:

_____

_____

_____

_____

_____

_____

_____

_____

ABOUT THE AUTHOR
DR. JACKIE ELDRIDGE

With many years as an elementary school teacher, teacher educator, university administrator, keynote speaker, workshop presenter and coach, Jackie is passionate about inspiring people to be the best they can be so they will be agents of change. Jackie is a co-creator of the internationally recognized professional development company Hearts and Minds Matter. Her work there is grounded in her belief that living, learning, and working environments must be safe, nurturing communities where people have what they need to thrive and grow.

Jackie believes that all people can make a difference in the world when they are able to tap into their own understanding of self and others. Jackie's doctoral research on the ethics of care, demonstrates her core value of the importance of caring connections in all of life's relationships.

Jackie also teaches in the Master of Teaching Program at the Ontario Institute for Studies in Education at the University of Toronto where she teaches The Fundamentals of Teaching and Learning. Additionally, she offers workshops and courses in emotional intelligence, resilience, mindfulness, growth mindset and personality dimensions.

Jackie is a co-author of *Hearts and Minds Matter: Creating Learning Environments Where All Students Belong and* the author of *Mindfulness: 15 Tips to Get You Started.*

Both are available at www.heartsandmindsmatter.com.

Jackie is currently writing The Emotional Intelligence Journal and the accompanying Emotional Intelligence Intention cards for adults and for children as well as a new educational text entitled: *Trauma-Informed Classrooms: Hearts and Minds Really Matter.*

Contact Jackie at jackie@heartsandmindsmatter.com

CPSIA information can be obtained
at www.ICGtesting.com
Printed in the USA
LVHW041203011221
705871LV00014B/1/1
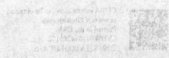

CPSIA information can be obtained
at www.ICGtesting.com
Printed in the USA
LVHW042044260122
709482LV00014B/436